Tales of Inner Strength and Spiritual Values

Tales of Inner Strength and Spiritual Values

By

Uma Chopra

KALPAZ

ISBN : 978-93-8022-234-9

Price : ₹ 125/-

First Published 2014

Published by

Kalpaz Publications
C-30, Satyawati Nagar,
Delhi-110052
Ph. : 9212142040
E-mail: kalpaz@hotmail.com

Laser Typesetting : Shubham Printers, Delhi
Printed at : G. Print Process, Delhi

Cataloging in Publication Data—DK
Courtesy: D.K. Agencies (P) Ltd. <docinfo@dkagencies.com>

Chopra, Uma.
Tales of inner strength and spiritual values / by Uma Chopra.
p. cm.
Short stories.
ISBN 9789380222349

1. Chopra, Uma—Childhood and youth—Anecdotes. 2. Chopra, Uma—Family—Anecdotes. 3. India—Anecdotes. 4. Short stories, Indic (English). I. Title.

DDC 823.92 23

ACKNOWLEDGEMENT

These stories are written for her son Sameer Chopra and are dedicated unhesitatingly to her mother and father as their valuable guidance and inspiration make an impact to write this book. She thanks her husband Surinder Kumar Chopra; without his co-operation, this book would not have been possible.

PART I–TRUE STORIES

AN UNFORGETABLE PERSONALITY - "BIJI"

My first impression of my *dadiji* are scary yet admirable. When I was a child, I was in awe of her strong personality. I loved her so much but was also suitably scared of her. I admired her courage, determination and her tremendous sense of humour. She was one person I knew who had the temerity to face any kind of problem with ease.

Kamlavati Marya, was a distinguished social worker in Patiala and was suitably awarded a medal for her good activities, by the Red Cross. As a child, I remember being very proud of her. Whatever little social work or charities I may have done in my life were inspired by her indomitable spirit and my mother's support.

She was so bold that nothing could dampen her spirit for very long. I have thought in my mind so many times that she was something like the phoenix that reincarnates from its ashes. She also had the capacity and the strength of mind to do just that with her life.

She was blessed with six sons, and she used to run a huge establishment. She was always found to be seen by the side of her husband through thick and thin.

She died at the age of eighty-seven. I remember her tell her family members on so many occepsions, "please give me an injection of Morphia before you take me to the cremation grounds because the fire otherwise will be very painful."

She was always seen in a smiling mood and made everybody around her laugh. When we were children we all looked forward to our Biji's visits because we knew she would give us a good time. She bubbled over with *joie de vivre.*

In her younger days she knew how to swim and horse riding. We were told that she was once riding on a horse cart when it fell into a canal. Not only did she swim to safety but she also rescued the other passengers.

Her courage was admirable in the family. My grandfather went to England to study medicine, leaving her behind with four little sons with no source of income. Whatever income my grandfather had was made the he spent towards his educational expenses. It did not discourage her, nor was she bogged down under the pressure. Instead, she used the milk from the family's dairy farming in order to manage her family.

When her husband returned from England, he was appointed as the civil surgeon and so had no time for anything except serving the ailing patients. It was she who managed the family's entire estate. She could not get formal education because of an early marriage, but that did not deter her from anything she wanted to do.

One thing that I couldn't forget about her when she suffered from a paralytic stroke. She was alone in the village when it happened. She at once realised that it was something serious and without wasting time she hired a taxi and went to her son, who is a doctor.

She recovered but her left side became very weak due to that reason. It was through good medical exercise and her indomitable will, she overcame her disability. She started moving around with the help of a walker in the house and managed to do everything on her own.

I would always remember my grandmother with the utmost affection and admiration. She was undoubtedly one of the most outstanding personalities in my life. She derived her strength from her strong will power. If we could follow the same kind of spirit in our life as she did the world would be a much better place to live in.

MANHUS GAURI

Gauri was a very beautiful woman endeared with all the good qualities.

She was a young girl, aged barely fourteen when she got married. She came to this village, situated in the far interior of old Bihar, surrounded by lush green fields and having a population of hardly two hundred people.

She arrived in the conventional carriage used for brides during those time—a *palki* covering with red flowing curtains so that anybody couldn't see her from outside. Her husband was two years her senior. One could say that she was happy with him. They were very poor, having one small hut as a house and maybe an acre of land to eke out a living.

The husband had a younger brother and an old mother to look after. The girl, despite the extreme hardships and poverty, bloomed into a beautyful woman and became the eyeshore of the village belles. Her husband, though a good man, became very insensitive and gave her orders to observe strict *purdah*.

At twenty-four she was still childless. This was considered to be a badomen, and could bring extreme calamity for the household. The old women of the village, with a cruel glint in their eyes, started advising the mother-in-law and the husband as to the non-suitability of a barren woman as a wife and a daughter-in-law. *"What is a woman worth if she couldn't bear a child?"* The husband become harsh and cruel. He took a threatening stand: "I will take another woman as my wife. I want children. What am I to do with beauty? You have become like a mill stone round my neck."

He abused her and beat her. When her husband was very angry he would even spit on her face. Nobody intervened. The remaining family members behaved with cruelty to add to her misery.

When she was barely thirty her husband died. The funeral followed by rituals were over. She got no sympathy. Everybody called her *manhus* - unlucky. They even went to the extent of accusing her of being the cause of her husband's death. She had to remain with her in-laws because her parents and family refused to take back her despite knowing about the ill-treatment, given by in-laws.

The brother-in-law, though younger than her, wanted her because of her good looks. But she refused his advances she got thrashings but nobody came to rescue her. The women were jealous and envious. The villagers smirked, since they all had lewd thoughts and wanted to use her.

The mother-in-law was too old and gutless to oppose her son. A helpless Gauri was finally forced to give in to her brother in-law's rapacious desires. The village folk again reverted to their favourite pastime of harassing her. They would abuse her when she walked down the road. Nobody cared to peep at her broken heart. And she knew nobody would. More misery awaited her.

First the mother-in-law died; then her brother-in-law, due to cirrhosis of the liver caused by drinking too much.

Gauri was now alone and a mature woman of forty. Growing age had added grace and dignity to her carriage. The sorrow which had befallen her had lent a calm approach, which heightened her classical beauty.

But there was to be no respite. Now, she was alone in a hostile village. The more she was crushed, the more they labelled her as a *manhus* and shunned her. The men hounded her. One night she was raped. In the morning, *she knew that nobody would pay any need to her plight so she remained silent.* Yet, they started blaming her.

God has strange ways. This time she conceived and was soon expecting a child. Gauri's heart had been shattered. Her spirit had been broken. She knew that now the village people would lynch her finding no other way she thought of committing suscide. There was a well behind her hut. In the dead of night, she tied a large stone with her feet and jumped into the well. Her body was found the next morning. When her dead body was taken out, the villagers realised that she was pregnant at the time of her death. It was only then that the peoples perception about her changed. Whatever sympathy her death aroused was too late for Gauri. Her body was taken to the crematorium *ghat*. The entire village turned up. They all stood there with their eyes downcast.

Callousness, disgust, sadism and inhumanity; these are few of the ways, the cruelty shows its face in today's society." We live in a cruel society and till the time we cannot accept this in all honesty, we can never rectify any of the wrongs being perpetuated within our society.

"Gauri is dead. By ending her life she opened the real face of society. She leaves behind a legacy of sorrow, A burden we have to bear."

THE BRAHMIN FAMILY

The story is real and is of contemporary settings. I have changed all the names and locations for specific reasons.

A very pious, orthodox *Brahmin,* his wife and four children lived in Delhi peacefully. They were financially well-off because the *Brahmin* was in government service. He had left the traditional means of livelihood for a *Brahmin* and opted for service. Nevertheless, he was very religious and brought up his family in the old traditions. His eldest child was a girl, and when she was barely thirteen years of age, he arranged her marriage in a suitable and orthodox *Brahmin* family.

The girl had very little education. She continued to live with her parents as she would be sent to her husband's house only when she turned eighteen. As luck would have it, before she could be sent to her in-laws, her husband was attacked by some dreaded disease and died.

Consequently, calamity descended on the *Brahmin* family. As we are all aware that a Hindu widow has to live a life of rigid austerity. The girl child did not even know her husband and still she was to he his widow. Calamity of calamities—the father of the girl could not digest this tragedy which had be fallen on his daughter and he died of a heart attack.

Now, there were two younger brothers, a sister and the mother. The mother's heart was broken after the twin tragedies. The eldest son of the late Brahmin was not very responsible by nature, so Anil, the younger son, took charge of the family. He was then studying in the eighth class. The first thing he did was to convince his own family and relatives that *Didi* must not to go to the in-laws'house in order to stay with them. Against great opposition, he managed to persuade everybody.

This was the first step. Then the next fight he took on himself was to settle his *Didi* again. There was an insurmountable wall of orthodoxy and tradition but he did not back down. He launched his attack on society. He convinced his own brother, mother and sister of what he wanted to do. He won over the support of his immediate family. The brother and sister advertised in the papers for a suitable match. God helped them and there was a reasonable response. They personally went to meet the people concerned and met the boy, apprising him of the entire background of the girl. They then arranged a meeting between the boy and the girl. The boy agreed. The marriage was arranged and performed.

Anil was at the forefront to do everything. He had succeeded in re-settling his *Didi*. He was only in the eleventh standard.

His *Didi* went on to have children and was happily settled. She continues to live a happy life with her husband and children thanks to her brother Anil's fighting spirit and love for her.

This was not the end of his family's ordeal. This family somehow seemed to have a curse on it.

The younger sister grew up and got good education but she decided against getting married. She had seen so much drama in real life that is why she was averse to the idea of marrying.

By now Anil completed his graduation in engineering and went to England for doing some business. He started his own business and got a good success. Asha, the younger sister, helped him in the business and lived on in India with her mother and elder brother's family. The elder brother did nothing; he became an alcoholic and used to drink a lot. He had two children from his wife—one son and one daughter. His wife sacrificed her interests and lived only to bring-up her children, fully supported by Asha in maintaining the family. Anil looked after all of them by giving his full support.

Time passed by. The elder brother died, because of his excessive drinking habit. He succumbed to a serious liver problem. The old mother could not tolerate these tragedies and within a year of her son's demise she also passed away. The daughter-in-law and Asha gave her full treatment during her illness but couldn't save her.

Now, we come to Anil, the mainstay of the household. He got married to an English girl and established himself as a successful businessman his sister Asha looking after the Indian market and he managed it in England. But misfortune refused to leave them. Anil's wife developed bone cancer. They now did not know how long she would service and left her on God's mercy. Anil was looking after his entire family and dotted on his wife. He didn't want to have any children so he sacrificed his own interest so that he could bring-up his elder brother's children by giving them full support.

The interesting point was that despite facing all these series of setbacks, they continued to believe in the ultimate reality with faith and confidence—truly a devoted Indian Joint family and for that Anil deserved praise for his humane nature.

REINCARNATION

"Even as the attainment of childhood, youth and old age is to one in this physical life, so is the change to another body (at death) for the embodied soul. Wisemen are not deluded by this." This is a stanza from the Srimad Bhagvad Gita translated into English by Swami Tapasyanandaji. Here, Bhagwan Sri Krishna told Arjun that the *atman* is immortal; only the body is subject to birth and death.

This stanza forms the mainstay of the theory of reincarnation explained in Hindu scripture. Other religions scoff at it, but there have been instances where people have remembered their past lives.

I will discuss two such instances which I have experienced in my life. One is about my mother's sister and one is about my father's brother.

First, I will tell you about my *Masi* who, I was told, was about five when she remembered her past life. She was born in Calcutta; for some reason the family went to Lahore before partition. There, I was told, she was walking with her mother one day when suddenly she stopped and pointed towards a house. She said that that was where she was born in her previous life. She gave the names of her previous parents and her own name. She even said that she had died of small pox at the age of eleven. Her mother at first thought it was the imagination of the young girl and scolded her by saying 'just stop this nonsense'. But when the child very emphatically related her past life, my *naniji* became curious and just to check the story went back to that house. There she enquired from those, who were staying in that house. The names of the people my *masi* revealed to them. They said that they had moved from that house. But the present inhabitants of the house confirmed that there had been a death and the girl had died of small pox. She was then eleven years old. Even the names were confirmed.

The second incident was that of my *chachaji*. It was not as graphic as the above instance, but he too remembered his past life. He was a child of two or three years of age. My grandfather was searching for a diamond tipped knife for cutting glass. He could not locate it and he kept saying that his father definitely had it. Suddenly, this young boy called his grandfather by name, saying, "Nath, look for the knife on that self above that cupboard. I had kept it there." The shelf was on top even for my grandfather it was difficult to reach. The knife was found there, surprisingly. In addition, this child used to call his grandmother by her first name as if he was addressing his wife.

In both these instances, we discovered that, when we grow-up, we forgot the previous memories. This also proved what the Gita says. That does not mean that we did not take birth earlier.

"PUARIYAN"

Puariyan is a word, used to indicate a person's clinical death before once again returning to life. It means 'a person was declared dead medically but at the time of his funeral, He suddenly got back his or her life to leave everybody in a state of surprise.

As a child I heard this word being used quite often. Once, out of curiosity, I asked Gyaso Devi, my *ayah*, all about it. She said that she herself had been a living example of *puariyan*. I was agog and pleaded with her to tell what had happened to her.

At I was requesting her to tell of her experience. She narrated to me that when she was in her forties. She said that she was very young at that time and was a mother of two sons.

Apparently, one day she was working in the fields and developed fever. She was brought home and all efforts were made to cure her of the malady but to no avail. The high temperature did not lessen and one day, she died with all of her dear and near ones surrounding her. But she could see her dead body was lying on the floor and everybody was crying. She tried to tell them that at that time she was alright but nobody could see or hear her.

She went on to tell that she started rising upwards and came to a place where an old man with a long beard was going through a register. He called out her name and when she answered, he looked at her and once again consulted the book. Then he shook his head and told one of the attendants that a serious mistake had committed. This was not the same Gyaso Devi who was to die today as per his account. He immediately told the man that this Gyaso Devi was to leave a long life and that arrangements should be made immediately to return her soul to her subtle body, means her physical body before it was burnt.

My *Ayah* told that she had to leave from there at once as if someone pushed her from a great height and she felt down with a jolt. When she woke up, she was in her own body, and at that time the body was being lifted to be taken to the cremation grounds. Then someone noticed that her foot was moving. Some person who knew of such things said that she was alive and that she had returned from the dead. Her body was put down and she was asked about whether she could remember anything. She narrated everything what had happened. Everybody was amazed and also happy to get her back.

Throughout I was spellbound, and my mouth remained wide open. I kept asking her whether it was true. Now, as a grown up adult, I have heard of a number of clinical deaths and the mysterious return of the person to life. And I know that medical science has no answers to this. Now, sometimes I feel that maybe what she told me at that time is very much possible.

A MOTHER'S LOVE

This incident which I am going to tell is about my father. My grand-father, Raghunath Singh Marya was a doctor of the Old Patiala State of pre-independence days, ruled by Maharaja Bhupinder Singh in the years 1923 to 1954. Raghunath Singh was married in 1916 to my grand-mother, Kamla Marya. They had six sons. My father Raj Kumar Singh Marya was their eldest offspring.

My grand-father wanted *papa* to follow in his footsteps. He wanted to make him a doctor. My father, on the other hand, was not inclined to pursue his career in medicine and wanted to be an aeronautical engineer. Aviation was considered to be very challenging in those days and few even knew about it. Grand-father enrolled him in Delhi in the year 1936 to study aviation but in 1937 or 1938, the institution closed down, so he sent *papa* to England to continue his studies in the same stream.

In August 1938, *papa* sailed for England on a ship named, Strathmore. On reaching, he joined his college to study engineering in the Midlands.

World War II started and all educational institutions closed down. *Papa* did not want to return to India without having achieved something in his life, so he enlisted his name as an airman in the Royal Air Force England in the year 1940.

He served throughout the war in England and continued to do his study and got his engineering certificates. Later he was determined to get his Commission as an officer in the Royal Air Force before returning home.

He returned to India in 1944 after receiving his Commission and getting the rank of a pilot Officer. He had got himself transferred to the Indian Royal Air Force and subsequently he was sent back to his own country.

This incident which I am writing about is a true story. Before he returned home, our family had no news of him for over six months. My grand-mother used to keep fast and prayed for the welfare of her son to such an extent that people started thinking that she had lost her mental balance.

As my grand-mother told me that one night she had a dream that a nun was holding a *diya* and shielding the flame from going out with her hand. She came across the sea and handed the *diya* to my grand-mother. When my grandmother narrated her dream to my grand-father in the morning he was surprised because grand-mother had never seen a nun in real life but he said nothing and remained silent.

They had no information about *papa* but he had come back to Bombay. I remembered it was on that day when suddenly my grandmother started shouting with joy that her son was safe and had come back to India. A miracle was taking place. My youngest uncle was fourteen years old at that time. The entire family rushed to her after hearing this. What they saw amazed them. Milk was flowing out of her breasts. Nobody could offer an explanation. My grand-father was a medical man and simply could not fathom what had caused this phenomenon.

It was only after a few days, we received a telegram confirming what grand-mother was repeating again and again that her Raj had come back and they had to believe in the miracle witnessed by them. My father eventually retired from the Air Force as Air-Vice Marshal in 1974. He is 77 years old now and believes that what he has achieved in his life, is due to of his mother's unflinching support, prayers and blessings.

CHACHI GONSA, BABA RAMZAN AND TULLI

I am going to write about the three Muslim personalities who served a very orthodox Hindu family. They were loveable and trusted by all and they, in turn, reciprocated their love in the same way. The first person, who was lovingly referred to as Chachi Gonsa by the sons of the household, was a Muslim woman.

As the story goes by, she married one of our ancestors, a Marya who was a poor relative of my great grand-father. At that time my great grand-father was a civil surgeon of then Pepsu State ruled by the Maharaja of Patiala.

When the marriage took place there was obviously a hue and cry by the Hindus as well as the Muslims but the wedding was done and nothing could be changed about it. My great grand-father told his Marya brother that since you married this woman, I would surely accept her as a bahu. His influence was such that there was nobody who could challenge his authority and accepted her into the family and that paved the way for all the Maryas falling into line.

After few years, as luck would have destined, the Marya brother died suddenly. His wife, now became a widow but given shelter in great grand-father's household. She became like a housekeeper, looking after the house and the six grandsons. She came to be known as Chachi Gonsa by them. They loved her for her loving ways with them and she doted on them. She had no children of her own.

The women of the house could be unmindful at times; for example my grand-mother would insist on burning coals being put into Chachi Gonsa's eating utensils to purify them. Chachi Gonsa would say, "Let her be, she is like that." Biji (my grandmother) in turn trusted and loved her in her own way and gave her complete charge of bringing up her sons. She remained in the household till her last breath as she was adored by all for her good human nature despite being a Muslim.

Now, I told about Baba Ramzan. He was like a valet to my grand-father. He used to assist the running of the household. It was Baba Ramzan's duty to collect my grand-father's pay from the treasury. At that time, the salary paid in silver coins. The jewellery was given to him by Biji to put in safe custody whose loyalty was unquestionable. They trusted him and he never let them down. When partition took place in 1947, he left for Pakistan because his entire family was leaving there, but he left his heart behind. When my grand-father was blessed with his first grandson in 1948, Baba Ramzan sent Rs. five as *shagun* from Pakistan. When my grand-father passed away in 1958, Baba Ramzan read about his death in the Urdu newspapers in Pakistan and wrote a tearful letter of condolence to my father who was the eldest son.

Lastly, we come to Tuli. He was my grandfather's driver and he used to drive Biji and my mother, who was a newly-wed at that time.

In 1947, one fixed day when he knew that the Hindu-Muslim riots were going to break out at a certain time, Biji wanted him to drive her around. He drove Biji and my mother till twelve noon, and then he brought them home. Biji was annoyed with him for doing so, but he disobeyed her which otherwise he never did. He gave the car keys to Biji and went away and never returned. The riots broke out within a short time after his departure.

The Hindu-Muslim rivalry which we talk about is purely political. Where hearts meet, only love remains; and only love is remembered.

One of my uncles, who is in his seventies now, always praises Chachi Gonsa, "No Hindu woman could be more god-fearing or devoted as she was she sacrificed her entire life for us brothers." and served the family with full dedication till her last breath to etch an inedible love on our heart.

THE NANGTA SADHU

This is a true incidence and it happened in pre-independence India. In Lahore, my *Naniji* was a young woman then. She gave birth to her two children: my mother, who was the eldest, and a younger brother. The gap between the two was barely a year. After these two, *Naniji* endured 11 years without conceiving another child.

One day, she was outside her house and doing some cleaning work when she saw a *Nangta* Sadhu standing in front of their gate. He was asking for some *Bhiksha* from her. As was the tradition, she brought out some coins and pulses and gave it to him. He blessed her and then said that since she was the first person who he had approached on that day, he wanted to do something for her. He asked her to bring out a *katori* and then told her to cover it with her *saree paloo*. He muttered some *mantras*. While he was doing this, my *Naniji* felt that the *katori* was burning hot and she could not hold it.

The Sadhu asked her to uncover it and not to put it down, and behold, the *katori* was full of burning red hot embers. My *Naniji* and her mother in-law were really amazed. They asked the Sadhu what was the meaning of this. He said that someone who was jealous of my *Naniji's* good luck had got some black magic done on her so that she would not have any more children.

He said that he had broken this evil and now after nine months my *Naniji* would give birth to a baby girl. This child, he said would be very "heavy" on her father, meaning that she would bring him bad luck.

After hearing this my *Naniji* was quite annoyed and asked him to leave. She was not prepared to listen to him anymore. Her mother-in-law asked the Sadhu what was to be done to mitigate this bad luck, but my *Naniji* could not hold her anger almost pushed the Sadhu out.

The Sadhu said this, as he was leaving, "you are not listening now. You would rue the day and search for me but you would not find me." And he left.

The mother-in-law lamented and scolded my *Naniji* for being so arrogant but *Naniji* paid no heed. The Sadhu's words come true. After nine months, my *Naniji* gave birth to a girl and my *Nanaji* lost his job. They went under severe financial losses. Now, my *Naniji* searched all over Lahore for that *Nangta* Sadhu but she could find no trace of him. Again his words came true.

The daughter suffered a number of reversals and remained a spinster all her life. Some things such as this happen in life which have no logical explanation.

SATI MA

This is a very controversial subject and does not hold any importance in the present context and rightly so. However, in this particular case I will only relate what actually happened then it is up to the readers.

This story unfolded in a village of the Punjab named Talwan. There lived a very pious woman totally devoted to her husband. Now, this required a little explanation.

As we are all aware, in Hinduism all Hindus are supposed to have an *Isht Devata whom they worshipped.* Everybody has freedom to choose any form of deity that appeals to him and worship all his devotions to that one idol. The Hindu is also taught to develop a particular attitude towards God. One is encouraged to think of God as a friend, as mother or as father or as husband. Miraji dedicated her life to Krishna Bhagwan and treated him as her husband.

From time immemorial the Hindu woman was taught to consider her husband as God and worshiped him as her *Isht*. If we can worship God in a clay image, then why not as a living being? This particular lady had such an attitude towards her husband. It is said that through such an approach she developed spiritually.

Time went on and then one day that ladys husband passed away. She decided to offer her body, and burn herself with the body of her husband. This happened during the British Raj and was about the same time that *sati* had been legally banned. The people of the village tried to discourage her but she did not listen to anybody.

Her husband's body was put on the funeral pyre. The woman sat down on the pyre with her husband's head on her lap. She asked the villagers to light the fire but nobody came forward because they were scared of being punished due to the banning of Sati pratha. Then she said that she would light the fire herself, but again nobody gave her fire. It was said that from her own hand fire sparked out and the funeral pyre was suddenly lighted in flames. Her live body was burnt along with her husband.

Again this requires a little explanation. One has heard innumerable times that a saint or a highly spiritually evolved person went into *Maha Samadhi* and left his body. This lady also did the same to show her total devotion to her husband.

Till today, I believe that in Talwan, people worship her as a saint and make offerings before her *samadhi*. They say that if you pray with a pure mind then what you want you can get. To this day, she is known as *Sati Ma* and is worshiped as a saint.

A WIFE'S SACRIFICE — A TRIBUTE

Once there lived a famous medical practitioner. He had a sound social standing. He was a well-known doctor of that area and a very rich man. He had a wife whom he loved very much. He had everything like money, fame and position. He only lacked of one thing as he did not have any children of his own.

The couple used to keep fasts and prayed for progeny but their prayers were not answered. The man was reconciled to giving away all his wealth and belongings to others. His wife, who was a good-natured woman, understood her husband's mental condition.

After a great deal of thought and introspection, she came to a conclusion. She would give up her husband for his welfare. She asked him to get married again. His husband was flabbergasted but she managed to persuade him. She went to a family she knew, who had an eligible girl. She went and asked for her hand from her parents for her husband and assured them that she would step out of their lives and give up all her marital rights which she enjoyed as his wife.

The marriage took place and she, true to her word, went away to the village home. The rest of her life she spent there, except two months in the year when she returned to her husband. This too because she was an asthmatic and during harvest time she could not stay in the village. She stayed as a guardian and a well-wisher of her husband's family till the very end.

The husband, because of her great sacrifice, was blessed with a son and two daughters. He held her with high regard and so did all the family members.

This is a true occurrence and due to her sacrifice her husband got children and lead a happy life. They owe their happiness to this great lady. How many women are there in today's society like her, who not only saved her husbands life but also gave progeny through her sacrifice. She deserved praise for that really.

A TRUE STORY

I have changed the names of the characters but the location and the essence of the story remains unchanged.

This incident happened in a remote village of the Punjab called Talwan. The time of this story is set during the British Raj–between the end of the 19th century and the start of the 20th century.

A good, well-to-do family had two sons. The elder son Gopal was sent to America to an engineer since in those days India did not have adequate educational facilities. When Gopal came back, he got the post of Overseer. This was one of the higher posts offered by the Britishers to the Indians. Badal, the younger son, was also later sent to America for higher studies.

Gopal married and settled down. He had five children within a short period of time. Now, as an Overseer, it was part of his duty to go on inspection of the surrounding areas and ensure that water was being fairly distributed among the farmers. One day a complaint came from an adjoining village that a farmer had cut off the supply of another farmer and was watering his own fields. Gopal set forth on his horse to set matters right. When he reached the location he found the complaint was valid. He went into the village to accost the culprit. He found him seated under a huge banyan tree. He was wearing a white *kurta pyjama* and a light pink *pagari* on his head, and was smoking a *hukka*. The man, Kartar Singh, got up and respectfully greeted Gopal. Gopal accused him of having done wrong. Kartar Singh tried to bribe Gopal but did not succeed. He was sentenced to three years of rigorous imprisonment. He vowed to take revenge on Gopal.

Gopal forgot about the incident and continued to lead his life normally. Three years passed and Kartar Singh came out of prison.

He invited Gopal to come and be his guest. Gopal quite innocently accepted his hospitality.

It was said that at that time Kartar Singh gave Gopal *masan* mixed with sweetened rice to eat. *Masan* is the ash from a cremation ground with certain evil and very potent *mantras* charged within it. It is supposed to kill the person, who consumes it.

Gopal came home and after sometime his health deteriorated. All types of medication were tried but to no avail. Allopathic, Unani, Ayurvedic, Homeopathic-everything. His mother prayed and went from temple to temple. By this time Gopal's entire body had broken out in sores. His mother, out of desperation and after fighting with her husband because he did not believe in this "hours pours" as he termed it, went to a Baba. Baba took one look at Gopal's mother and said that she came to him too late. Nothing could be done now. Her son would die within three months on a particular day. He predicted his end. The mother came back crying and howling.

As predicted by the Baba, Goapl died after three months. But this is not the amazing part. The amazing part is that in America, his younger brother Badal had a vivid dream in which Gopal told him that Kartar Singh did it in vengeance and had killed him by feeding him *masan* in sweetened rice. In the dream, Gopal showed Kartar Singh was sitting under the banyan tree while smoking a *hukka* and wearing his white *kurta* pyjama with light pink *pagari.* However, Gopal made his brother promise that he would not in turn harm Kartar Singh because then Gopal's children would suffer.

When Badal returned to India, the first thing he did was to get on a horse and went out to the village to see for himself if his dream was true or not. His mother tried to stop him but he did not listen.

When he entered this village, he saw exactly what he had seen in the dream—Kartar Singh was sitting under the banyan tree, smoking a *hukka* exactly in the manner which he saw in his dream.

What Badal saw verified his dream and by now his mother and other relatives had also told him what had transpired. Badal returned home a much saddened and sober man.

Now, Badal realised that what he saw in his dream was true. He told this to his mother and relatives and the main reason of premature demise of his elder brother. But Badal did not take revenge as it was advised by his late brother to set a precedent. "Hate is not conquered by hate, hate is conquered by love".

THE 'BEWITCHED' GIRL

I am narrating this incident as told to me by my mother. This story took place in Kurali, a remote village of Punjab where my *Naniji* (maternal grandmother) was born and brought up. It is situated in the near vicinity of Chandigarh; however, at the time of this happenings, Chandigarh did not exist.

On the outskirts of this village there was a huge banyan tree which was believed to be inhabited by a *Dayan*, an evil female spirit. People in fear avoided going anywhere near this tree, leave alone passing under it.

One day, a young girl who was nearly twelve years of age put on a pink veil, applied perfume and, in defiance of all the elders, decided to pass under that prohibited tree. In India, we believe that the evil spirits love colour and perfume. This girl was wearing both. She defiantly walked under the tree and then walked back home without any mishappening.

On reaching home, she told her mother that she was very hungry. That day, because of a festival in the family, special food–milk *payasam* and *puri*-had been cooked. The mother gave the girl some to eat. The girl kept praising the food and kept eating and asking for more. Eventually, all of the food which was to be fed by one family was devoured by this child. Then she said that she was thirsty. The mother gave her some *sherbet*, which was also consumed by the girl.

The mother and the elders of the family were amazed and were petrified They all felt that *Chacha*, an elderly man who knew about spirits, should be consulted immediately.

Chacha hastened to the spot and chanted a few *mantras*. He said that the evil spirit which resided in the tree had entered the girl's body and was vicariously enjoying the food and drink.

Now, the entire village had gathered and all pleaded with *Chacha* to do something and save the girl from the clutches of this evil influence.

Chacha marked a circle in which he sat and said some prayers. He chanted *mantras*. The spirit became restless and begged him to stop. The old man said she must leave the girl's body and go away. The spirit agreed. *Chacha* wanted some proof from the spirit that she was leaving the body of the victim. He said that the tree standing in front of the girl's house should break when you (spirit), would leave. The evil influence agreed. All were present and all of a sudden the tree snapped into two. The spirit had departed and the girl fell to the floor unconscious. She was revived and made to rest. After that incident the said girl lived a trouble-free life, got married and lead a happy life with her family.

This occurrence is still repeated in that village to make children obey their elders and not to be defiant.

REAL WOMEN

Panditaniji, Kamal Marya, and Gyan Khosla

These women with many parts who were very closely interlinked with my life and I knew them intimately. Each of them got some qualities to lead their lives in their own way.

When I got the chance of meeting Panditaniji, she was already an old woman. Her built was short stature with a fair complexion and a very wrinkled face. But there was something in her face and eyes which attracted everybody.

The story which I related earlier about *Sati Ma* has a special meaning for her as Panditaniji came from the same village and worshipped *Sati Ma*. She had made *Sati Ma* her *Isht*.

Panditaniji had been widowed at the very young age and was a poor *Brahmin* lady. It was said that she did intense penance, *tapasya* and was blessed with some powers. For example, she could foretell future events. She was the Panditaniji of all the Khoslas. They gave her in cash and kind; she, in turn, prayed for their welfare.

What amazed me about her was that even at the age of ninety, she could do so much work. She seemed to radiate love and well being. There was a warmth which surrounded her and one could sense it as a tangible thing. She lived in extreme poverty but never asked any help from anybody. She was kind and generous, whoever went to her was welcomed and offered whatever she had to eat. One felt a sense of peace after giving something in the exchange of getting her blessings.

Her death was very quiet and gentle. She passed away in her sleep, chanting the name of her *Sati Ma*. That was the end of her story but she led a saint's life throughout. The people she knew even remembered her with love and respect.

Kamala Marya was my *Dadiji.* Since my very childhood, I admired her for her immense courage and spirit. She was an extrovert. As a child she learnt how to swim and to ride a horse. This is almost over a hundred years ago. Women at that time were restricted and not given a free-hand.

My Dadiji got married at the age of fifteen or sixteen. Her husband doted on her and they were blessed with six sons. Now, when I have one son of my own and I have to take lot of pains in his up-bringing, I am amazed at her being able to bring-up six sons without any problem.

She dressed very well. She got very little formal education but that did not defer her as she went on to become the President of the Red Cross in Patiala and was honoured for her extraordinary spirit and determination.

She died when she was eighty-seven. Ten years before her death, she got a paralytic stroke. As a result, her left side became very weak, but that did not get her down. She walked with the help of a walker and travelled across the country. She used to look after herself right till the end despite her poor health. She knew exactly how much money she had in the bank and how much interest was due and when; which showed how alert, she was.

My grandfather was a very busy doctor and did not have the time to look after the affairs of his family, land and other activities, so she (Biji) took over. She looked after the farms and the other properties.

She had a zest for life. Nothing could bog down her spirit. She never gave up. She had a brilliant sense of fun and used to make people laugh around her. She was truly an adorable person.

Gijan Khosla was my *Naniji.* She reminded me of a rock. She was a pillar of strength. She ruled her family with an iron hand. Nobody could dare to speak in front of her. But she was a God-fearing woman and she made tremendous sacrifices in her life.

In 1947, she brought home an orphan boy whom she educated and looked after as her own child.

Sometimes I used to wonder where she got such inner-strength from. Her strength was her prayers. She used to get up at 3 a.m. and pray for five hours, and she prayed throughout the day. At the time of doing some work she used to do her *japa.* She died at the age of 92. Two years before her death she used to work in the kitchen. But in the last two years of her life she suffered a lot but she endured it without complaint or grumbling. She was truly a woman of very strong character who drew respect and admiration. What I learnt from these three women was that there is tremendous strength within oneself that one should be able to inculcate. And somehow it inspired me that all three of them were very spiritually-minded. Every time they faced an adverse circumstance, they turned to God and managed to overcome their problems with remarkable ease.

A MOTHER'S CURSE

Talwan is a village, situated in Punjab. The story I want to narrate happened near this village in the early part of the 20th century.

In this village, there lived a very well-respected woman. She was popularly known as Grandmother. She was very pious and she was a firm believer in God. It was believed that she attained a certain spiritual evolution through her deeds, penance and rigid austerity.

She had a son who was married and the father of three children, two sons and a daughter. Her son did not get along with his wife because she was a very simple, uneducated woman. Years went by and his discontentment must have deepened. Eventually, he went to the city and there met a another woman whom he decided to marry.

When his mother heard that her son wanted to get married again, she took her daughter-in-law and went to persuade her son and requesting him not to do this. All her entreaties fell on deaf ears. The son was determined to marry again.

The mother then drew her *saree* veil over her face and cursed the son that from this moment onward, he was dead for her. He was doing great injustice to his first wife who was mother of his own children. He had no business to subject her to this humiliation just because she was simple and did not have sophisticated ways. She further said that she took away his right to light the funeral fire to her body after her death. She went on to say that her grandchildren would flourish but he himself would die in an extreme poverty. Then she turned to her daughter-in-law and asked if she still wished to continue living with her husband, or would she chose to go with her to the village home.

The daughter-in-law followed her mother-in-law and made her home in the village to lead a peaceful life with her kids.

In the meantime, her two sons and daughter grew up. The daughter got married into a good family. The two sons bacame qualified engineers. And, as the grandmother had predicted, they flourished. After four years her mother-in-law passed away. True to her word, she never again spoke to her son or saw him during her remaining life and told her at the time of death that her son should not be allowed to light her funeral pyre.

Time went on and her son lost everything. His second wife had no children and so, out of sheer frustration, she started wasting her husband's money. Eventually, when he died, there was no money left for his funeral. His sons from the first wife performed the funeral and rituals The curse which had given by his mother came true.

POOJARIJI

Here is a true incident which I am narrating to you. I heard this story from my mother. This incident happened in pre-Independence period, as our country was then under the British rule. Some states continued to be governed by the Indian Rajas under British protection. Two such states which we are going to talk about were the Punjab and a small neighbouring state of Nabha. Both were ruled by the kings at that time.

Over some dispute the Maharaja of Patiala and the Raja of Nabha had an altercation and the feud reached the courts. The Raja of Nabha would be reduced to penury if he lost the court case.

The Raja of Nabha had a *Diwan,* the Prime Minister, whom he relied upon a great deal, and the *Diwan in turn was totally loyal to his king. He knew of a great Shiva devotee Bhakt—a poojari* of the Shiv Temple. It was believed that this *poojari* had *darshan* of *Bhagwan* Shivji and he used to hold intimate conversations with him.

The *Diwan* turned to the *poojari* and pleaded earnestly him with him to do something for the state of Nabha, otherwise it would be destroyed.

On the day when the case was to be decided, the *Diwan* went to see the *poojari* in the Shiv Temple and was told that for the last two days, the *poojari* had shut himself in the sanctum sanctorum. The *Diwan* approached the temple and he could hear the *poojari* talking to someone. He was saying that if this court case is not decided in the Raja of Nabha's favour (bacause he was also in the right) he would kill himself. A voice was heard answering him, "why are you fighting with me so much? The king has won the case." Just then a messenger arrived on horse back to inform the *Diwan* that the judgement had been given in favour of the Raja of Nabha.

The *Diwan* now requested the *Poojari* to open the temple door to come out. When he did, to everyone's utter amazement, they found nobody inside except the *Poojari* himself. Presumably, the voice which all had heard was *Bhagwan* Shivji's. All fell on the *Poojari's* feet with great humility. This temple still stands and it is said that anybody who prays there with a pure mind gets what he desires.

HAPPENINGS

Here, I will tell two different incidents which to my knowledge are true.

The first one about how a surname came into existence. Incidentally, this surname was the one I was born with. It was my maiden name–Marya. In Punjabi, this name is pronounced as ड़.In English, it became Marya because the soundड़is missing from the English alphabet.

Now the wordमड़ियाMarya comes from the cremation ground...

As the story goes, an entire clan of our aseestors were wiped out during a war; only one woman survived and she was full-term pregnant. She also apparently was in bad shape and was declared also as dead. When she was taken to the cremation ground for the funeral, someone saw her stomach move. The child in her was still alive. They cut her stomach open and—miracle of miracles—a healthy baby boy was born. So, since that boy was born in the cremation ground, his name becameमड़िया. This, in turn, became Marya when written in English.

With the birth of the boy, a new surname also came to the being. This is the reality behind my maiden surname. I was told this story by my mother.

The second happening is from my maternal side of the family. My mother told me about this as she had personally experienced it.

Talwan was a village where all the Khoslas stayed. Khosla was my mother's surname before she married my father. There stood the family *haveli*, old and majestic. In the innercourtyard of the *haveli* there was a wooden *dewan*. This *dewan* was used by my mother's grandmother (*dadiji*) for doing her daily *puja*. It was said that every day at 3 a.m., the grandmother, after her ablutions, would sit on the *dewan* and do her *japa* and meditation. This practice went on throughout her life. Now, it is believed that even after her death, she continued to pray on that *dewan* at the scheduled time in the early hours of the morning. Nobody dared to sleep on that *dewan* because if they did, they were rudely awakened by a slap and a voice ordered them to leave the *dewan* since it was time for her *puja*.

When my mother was a teenager, she refused to believe the story. On one of her visits to the family home, just to put the above fact to test, she slept on the *dewan*. She said that sometime at the dead of the night, since she did not have a light or a watch with her to see the time, she was rudely awakened by somebody shaking her hand and a voice asked her to get up. She said she remembered it clearly and never again dared to sleep on that *dewan* after that incident.

THE TRUTH

This is a true occurrence. I am merely elucidating the facts so as to incite awareness and, as a result, hope that in the future, some action may be taken against such people. It is our society which permits such atrocities to go unpunished merely because nobody is prepared to involve themselves in a controversial topic like dowry. We seem to have become hardened to hearing about dowry victims. "Do you know she was burnt by her in-laws because she brought insufficient dowry?" or "Her husband beats her on the instigation of his mother because she has not brought enough cash." The most that happens is that we shake our heads and cluck in disapproval and then the conversational topic is changed to movies, politics or real estate. Anything to get away from the problem of finding a solution. The worst is that girls are expected to carry on with their marriages. The question of the girl breaking her marriage because of dowry demands is frowned upon till it is too late.

It happened to Sheila. She comes from a middle class family. The parents saved and collected things for their daughter to give her away in marriage when the appropriate time came. The time came and she was married amidst all the rejoicing, pomp and glory which her parents could afford. The bride looked forward with starry eyes to her new life. Her husband was an engineer and was stationed abroad. A week after the marriage, Sheila's bubble burst. The husband, without her consent or concurrence, handed over her entire possessions to his parents. The explanation given was that since they were going out of the country, it would be difficult to cart her things with them.

The second week brought another disillusionment. The in-laws and the husband wanted her to get another Rs. 15,000/- in cash from her parents. She had to do this if she wanted to accompany her husband to the States. This time the excuse was his inability to pay for her ticket as he did not have sufficient funds.

This is the time when her parents should have put their foot down, but that did not happen. They paid the money, hoping that it would result in their daughter's happiness.

Sheila's unhappiness increased because the husband was now treating her with the utmost indifference. Apparently, he was not keen on taking her with him. Pressure and persuasion were brought to bear on him from her parents until he, most reluctantly, concurred to her accompanying him.

The day of departure came. Sheila was allowed to pack the minimum of her clothes; the remainder was distributed to her two sisters-in-law. Sheila wanted to object, but was hushed by her parents. They hoped that the marriage would stabilise once the couple went abroad. Sheila kept quiet but the stars had gone out of her eyes.

The final blow was yet to come. They landed and he took her to his flat. He decided to be frank with her. She was told point blank that he was already married and the father of two sons, aged seven and five. When asked why he had married her, he shrugged indifferently and explained that his parents wanted money. So he had carried out their wishes by supplying them with her dowry. And the parents were in the know about his first marriage. The husband magnanimously stated that she could continue staying with them as a domestic help.

Sheila, totally broken by now, rang up an uncle of hers who happened to be stationed in the near vicinity. He came and took her away.

Sheila returned to her parents, disillusioned and embittered. At present she is trying to pick up the threads of her shattered existence.

The culprits have escaped with nothing more than a few disapproving clucks from society. It is Sheila's life which has been ruined. She has completely lost confidence and trust in humanity.

The question to be answered is this: should such cases be allowed to go unpunished? Unfortunately, this is what happening and we as a society are to blame for that.

THE *BHAKT*

This is a story of two men. One of them was a great devotee of Lord Shiva and used to go every day to a Shiva Temple to offer his prayers situated on a mountain top, difficult to approach because of the thorny way. There daily he offered flowers and *Ganga Jal* to Bhagwan Shivji.

The other man was an atheist and did not believe in God, but he also went every day to the same Shiva Temple to throw stones at the altar in the same temple. This process went on for a long period of time. Both visited the Shiva Temple regularly.

Then one day there was heavy thunder. The storm raged in all its fury. The devotee looked at the weather and said, "This is not a conducive day to go out for offerings his prayers. The atheist, on the other hand, braved the storm and the rain and as usual went and threw stones at the altar. He was about to go out of the temple when Bhagwan Shivji gave him *darshan*.

On seeing the Lord, the atheist's mind was instantly purified of all impurities and he bowed reverently before Shivji. He then asked the Lord a question, "You have given *darshan* to one who came only to abuse you and throw stones at you. Why?" *Bhagwan* Shivji answered, "The other man, my devotee, did not brave this unusual weather. His devotion was not that intense, but you came even on this day. You were thinking of me constantly and your mind was on me even though the attitude was hostile. This constant thinking of me purified you and as a result, I am before you. Ask whatever boon you desire."

The atheist, who now totally transformed and converted to being a believer and a devotee, bent down to touch the Lord's feet and asked for only *Bhakti* devotion and nothing else.

TRUE OCCURRENCES

I am going to narrate two true occurrences which happened at different periods of time but are true.

The first one happened over a hundred years ago. This is about the birth of my *Naniji.* I believe that her parents did not have any children for a long time and in those days, progeny was very important and the entire blame for the lack of it fell entirely on the woman. Therefore, my *Naniji's* mother prayed resentlessly to *Bhagwan* Shivji for an offspring. She used to keep fasts and offered her prayers regularly to please the deity. I was told that her prayer was finally granted after eight long years of intense penance *tapasya.*

I was told that one night she fell asleep in front of the *Shiva Lingam* due to physical exhaustion. At night, Shivji appeared to her in a dream and said that he was very pleased with her devotion and she could ask for whatever she desired. She said that she wanted a child. He granted her a child but said that she would depart from this world at the time of giving birth to that child.

When my *Naniji* was born after a period of nine months, what her mother had dreamt came true. The child was born and her mother was also died instantly.

The second occurrence was with my own mother. She was about fourteen or fifteen years old at that time.

She told me that one day she was playing in front of her lawn when a Muslim friend of her father came. He was a very God-fearing man and obviously had some insight into future events. He asked my *Nanaji* about the girl child. *Nanaji* answered that she was his first born daughter.

That is when this man asked my *Nanaji* to do some prayers to be done regularly by my mother for the protection of her future husband. He said that on every Thursday, they should get a captive bird and keep it in a cage. My mother should feed it and give it water to drink and then set it free on the next Thursday. This process was to be repeated for seven weeks.

When my parents asked why this was to be done, he said that this girl's husband was flying around in the skies and this was to ensure that he came home to her safe without getting any injury to his body. At that time my mother was reluctant to do it, but because her father insisted, she complied with his request.

When she got married, it proved true as my father was in the Air Force and, as had been mentioned, he was in England and was flying over Germany, because the second World War broke out.

My mother could never really get over this Muslim man, who predicted this and its coming true. This was too much of a coincidence.

I want to share this with my readers about it because such things do happen in life and there is definitely a spiritual power guiding our destinies constantly and the entire universe too.

THE FAIRIES' DANCE

When we were children, my *Naniji* used to tell us one particular story which we all listened to with all our attention. We heard it from her over and over again. We could never have enough of it.

She said it was a true occurrence. It went something like this: I was a girl of ten years then, we lived in a small village in Punjab. My home was on the outskirts of the village. A little wood existed near my house. A small brook ran through it. In the daylight hours, we children would go to pluck wild flowers and berries and have a merry time there. It was a beautiful place, all green and peaceful, with birds twittering and squirrels coming down from the trees to gather nuts.

One day, I wandered a little deeper into the wood. That spot was even lovelier. The brook took a turn there. The clear waters gurgled. The waters were shallow. I waded through to the other side because I saw some beautiful flowers.

I plucked a few sweet smelling flowers then strangely I did not want to pick any more. That is when I noticed that the flowers made a perfect circle. I was very surprised. I looked around to see if anybody lived there, who could have planted these wildflowers like this. But there was no evidence of that. I looked again. Yes, the flowers made a perfect circle. I looked more carefully. This variety of flowers I had never seen before.

My friends started shouting for me. I ran towards them, not wanting to share this secret with them. I went home.

What a joy awaited me. My grandfather had come to visit us. He was supposed to know all about fairies, elves and pixies. I ran to him and hugged him. I showed him my flowers and then very confidentially told him about the perfect circle near the brook.

He looked at the flowers and said I should not have plucked these flowers. I told him, "Yes, Baba, I did not want to pick any more after taking a few." He said, "Show me this place tomorrow." I was only too happy to share my wonder place with him.

Tomorrow dawned. We both set out for our little adventure. Baba seemed excited. We reached the place in the little wood. I ran through the waters, pointing out the flowers to Baba.

He looked at the flowers. He walked around and nodded his head. I wanted to know what he was thinking. He said this is where the fairies came and danced on a *Purnima* (full moonlight) night. I looked at him with my eyes round and mouth open. "Fairies?" "Yes," he said, "Do you want to see their dance?" I could not believe my ears. When what he said sank in, I jumped up and down, clapping my hands, and I tugged at his *kurta*, "Baba, yes, please show them to me."

"Tomorrow is *Purnima*. At night, we will come here and at midnight you will see the fairies dance. But do not tell anybody else about it." I agreed. I would have agreed to anything then.

The day dawned after what seemed like a year to me. I had not slept at night. I did not know how I could wait till the night. Finally, we both sneaked out of the house and headed for the little wood. We reached the place. Baba stationed us behind a tree overlooking the circle of flowers. He sat down cross-legged and made me sit beside him. He took out his *japa mala* and closing his eyes, started doing *japa* of a certain *mantra*. (He told me this later on.) He said, "You cannot see them like this. I am chanting this *mantra* so that they became visible to you." I was excited and tense.

The place looked beautiful. Everything looked ethereal in the moonlight. I waited impatiently.

Baba said, "Quiet now," and touched me lightly on the forehead. I was absolutely still, virtually holding my breath. First I thought I was imagining. I looked at Baba. He smiled and with signs affirmed what I was asking him. I could hear music. I had never heard something like this before. Then suddenly before my eyes unfolded a scene. I can never forget, nor fully describe what I saw.

Fairies descended into that circle of flowers. They wore clothes which seemed to reflect the light of the moon. The whole place became aglow. I held my breath. For fifteen minutes after that, I was transported into a world of unknown. They danced to the musical strains of the divine music. Their steps were so light that it seemed they did not step on the ground. I could now vaguely understand what the *Raslila* must have been like. I cannot express the emotions arising within me at that time. The dance ended. The fairies vanished. The music stopped. Baba touched me on the shoulder and said, "Come"

We got back home. I could not sleep the whole night. The next morning I went to Baba. I wanted to confirm that what we had witnessed was not my imagination. He smiled and looked at me. It was all real. He said, "Now they will not dance there again." And nodded knowingly. "Even the circle of flowers will not be there."

I ran all the way back to see if he was correct. I crossed the brook and behold, as he had said, the flowers had also disappeared. It was all over, but the story of The Fairies' Dance has ever remained with me.

PART II - STORIES

THE PRINCE AND THE *RAKSHA*

Once upon a time, there lived a very powerful and dangerous *Raksha* on top of a mountain peak. He used to kill all, who came close to that mountain and then he devoured them to his heart content.

The king of that country was very worried about this. He found himself quite helpless and couldn't end the terror of *Raksha* So one day he made a declaration that whoever would be successful in killing the *Raksha*, he would give the hand of his beautiful daughter in marriage to him and also present him with half of his kingdom.

Nobody came forward because all were scared. One Prince of a small kingdom heard the story. He was very handsome and a very courageous man. He went to his father and said that he wanted to kill the *Raksha* but only after he saw the Princess for himself. The old king gave his son his blessings.

When the Prince approached the king he had taken a great liking to the noble and brave Prince. He said that he could not permit an official meeting with the Princess, but every evening she went for a stroll in the garden. The Prince, he suggested, should be in a beggar dress and could see his daughter in the garden.

The Prince was agreed. He disguised himself as a beggar and waited near the garden gate. When he saw the princess, he fell in love with her. As she was very beautiful. Now, he was determined to succeed in his mission.

He set out to find someone who could tell him more about the *Raksha*. He found out that about twenty miles away in a remote village lived an old man who could be of some help.

The Prince went to this old man and listened to him with great attention and then said that he had been waiting for him.

He further added that he got a 'magic sword' which he gave to the Prince. He told the Prince that he should cut off the *Raksha's* head with this sword at midnight on *Purnima*. The *Raksha* used to drink a lot of wine on that night after his heavy meal and fell fast asleep.

The Prince was very thankful to the old man but now he wanted to know how to approach the mountain.

The old man said that for this information, the prince would have to go to his younger brother who would be helpful.

The Prince mounted his horse and went to the village where the younger brother of the old man lived. When he reached the village, he was directed to a man sitting beneath a tree. He heard everything from Prince and then said, "you will have to approach the mountain from the back and then enter his cave and remain hidden there till the moonlit night." Then he gave the prince a magic ring and said that on reaching the mountain, he should call the fairy of the mountain. She would help him to accomplish his mission.

The Prince proceeded to the mountain. On reaching it, he called out to the fairy as that man had directed. In a twinkling of an eye, the fairy appeared in front of his eyes. Seeing the magic ring on the Prince's finger she asked him what she could do for him.

The Prince said he wanted to get inside the cave of the *Raksha* on *Purnima* night. She promised to help him in this.

On *Purnima*, the Prince called the fairy and she appeared. With a magic wand in her hand. She waved it thrice and then touched the Prince with it on his head. Within no time, the Prince found himself in the cave. He hid himself behind a rock.

As usual the *Raksha* had drunk a great deal of wine after a heavy meal and he fell fast asleep. At midnight, the Prince came out from hiding and cut off the *Raksha's* head with that magic sword. The *Raksha* was finished.

Now, the Prince took the head of the *Raksha* in a basket and went to the king. The king was overjoyed to know that the *Raksha* was no more. He declared the marriage of his daughter to the Prince and also gave him half of his kingdom.

The Prince and the Princess got married amidst a great deal of rejoicing with pomp and show. All were very happy as the tyranny of that dreaded *Rakhas* was ended. The Prince and the Princess lived happily ever after.

THE *RAKSHA* AND THE PRINCESS

Once upon a time, there lived a very cruel *Raksha*. He posed a serious threat to everybody. The people to that land were very disturbed and felt helpless at not being able to stop the *Raksha* from practising his wicked ways.

Nobody could harm him, leave alone kill him. The story went that the life of this *Raksha* was confined in a parrot and as long as the parrot was alive, nothing would happen to the *Raksha*. He kept the parrot very safe.

This was a boon given to the *Raksha* by the gods when he was a child and had done a great deal of *penance*. He had asked for immortality but the gods said that he would live as long as nobody killed the parrot.

As the years passed by, the cruelty of the *Raksha started* increasing. He had became so confident that he would live forever and become immortal.

One day, a king and his daughter were passing to that place where the *Raksha* lived. The Raksha saw the Princess. She was very beautiful, so he forcibly carried her away to his palace.

The Princess had a lovely voice and used to sing very well. The *Raksha* wanted the Princess to marry him. The Princess refused. The *Raksha* threatened to kill her and devoure her. The Princess resisted all his threats. The *Raksha* then gave the Princess an ultimatum. He said that every evening she would have to sing for him and the day she refused to sing, he would kill her.

The poor and helpless Princess did as she was told by the *Raksha*. Every evening she sang for the *Raksha*. She prayed for her release from this horrible captivity but to no avail.

One day, a handsome young man was passing near to the *Raksha's* palace. He heard the song that the Princess was singing for the wicked *Raksha*. He got curious and came nearer to see who was singing. He looked in through a window and saw the beautiful Princess was singing that song. He waited till the *Raksha* had gone to sleep and then he called the Princess to come near the window.

At first, the Princess was scared to talk to the young man, but then she gathered enough courage and went to the window. She told him her sad story and pleaded him to save her from the clutches of the *Raksha*.

The young man promised her that he would come in the morning when the *Raksha* was away and then told her about his plan.

In the morning when the *Raksha* went away, the Princess let in the young man who had been waiting outside. The man did not waste any time. He told the Princes that when the *Raksha* was in a good mood, she should try and get the secret of the parrot from him. Then he went away.

Now, when the *Raksha* returned home, the Princess was very nice to him and gave him wine to drink and cooked his favourite meal. She started singing and continued till he was quite drunk. Then she asked him about his immortality.

The *Raksha* was in a boastful mood and he told her that only when the parrot was killed then he would die. He also said that he had kept the parrot safe on a particular mountain on a tree. The way to identify the parrot from the others was that this parrot has blue wings. Then he fell asleep.

The Princess lost no time and gave the young man all the information. He left immediately for searching the mountain. On reaching there, he saw the tree and saw the parrot with the blue wings. He did not lose a moment and caught the bird. Then he twisted the parrot's neck at once. The bird died and then the *Raksha* fell down, never to get up again.

The Princess was finally out of his captivity and the land was freed from the tyranny of the *Raksha*.

The young man returned and safely took the Princess to the king. The king was overjoyed and gave the Princess in marriage to the young man. He also gave them a separate kingdom to rule over, and they lived happily ever after.

THE *GENIE* AND BEHARI

Once upon a time, there lived a magician who had captured a *genie* by his magic and kept him confined in a bottle. He made the *genie* to do all kinds of things for him. He treated him very badly. The *genie* was very unhappy.

One day, the magician took the bottle with him which held the *genie* and boarded a boat to cross the river to the other side. When the boat was in the middle of the huge river, a storm came up and overturned the boat. The magician drowned and died. The bottle floated on the waves and came to the shore where it stuck on the sand.

Behari, a boy of ten from a neighbouring village, was playing in the near vicinity of the bottle. He noticed this strange looking bottle and picked it up. He was curious to know what was inside the bottle so he opened the cork. Behold, the *genie* appeared out of the bottle and bowing reverently to Behari, he said, "What is your command, master? What can I do for you?"

Behari was amazed but kept his wits under control and asked the *genie* why he was confined in the bottle. The genie told him everything. Behari was a kind-hearted boy. He said that if the *genie* would promise to come whenever he was called, he would be set free him from this bottle. The *genie* was very glad and promised to do his bidding.

Behari went home. He came from a very poor family. His father had passed away when he was born. He lived with his widowed mother. He excitedly told his mother everything.

Behari had always wanted his mother to live in comfort. He called the *genie* and asked him if he could build a nice home for them and give them sufficient money so that his mother would not have to toil hard from morning till evening for making both ends, meet.

In the twinkling of eyes they had all that they had asked for and more from *genie*. Now, they started living in comfort and luxury.

Time passed by. Behari and the *genie* became true friends rather than having a master and slave like relationship.

Behari studied and learnt all kinds of arts and became a very accomplished lad. Now, Behari was a grown up young man.

One day, Behari told the *genie* that he would like to see the world. The *genie* was only too happy to oblige his kind friend.

The *genie* flew him from place to place and Behari was delighted to see the wondrous sights which unfolded before his eyes. They returned home after seeing the world. Behari was very restless. He was not satisfied. The *genie* asked him what was troubling him.

Behari said that when he was a boy, an old man had said that there was a place like a Fairy's Land. He had always wanted to visit that place. Please could the *genie* take him there?

The *genie* was taken aback. He tried to dissuade Behari because he said that human beings were not permitted in that land. But Behari did not like take no for an answer.

The *genie* had to obey. He held Behari by the hand and transported him to the Land of the Fairies. It was the most beautiful place that Behari had ever seen. Then he saw the Princess of the Fairies and he was stunned by her beauty. He had fallen deeply in love. On the other hand, when *Raslila* (the Princess) saw Behari, she surrendered her heart to him also. They both were drawn to each other and started meeting every day. The *genie* stood on guard. The two of them wanted to marry. Now, what was to be done?

Behari took the decision. He said that he would go and meet the king, irrespective of the consequences. *Raslila* and the *genie* were scared for him.

Behari set out the very next day to meet the king and narrated everything to him. When he reached the palace gates and asked for an audience with the king, all the fairies were amazed that how a human being could enter their realm.

Behari was presented before the king. The king asked him how could he manage to reach Fairy Land. Behari hid nothing and boldly told the whole story to the king. He ended by asking for Raslila's hand in marriage.

Normally, the king would have been furious but the king liked Behari's honesty and boldness. He said that a Fairy and a human being could not get married. It was not permitted. Raslila told her father quite honestly that she would marry Behari and nobody else. The king was in a dilemma. He could not understand what he should do. He was a very wise king and after thinking for a while, he said that only one thing was possible.

He said that Raslila should be permitted to go down to the mortal world with Behari and marry him there. She should stay with him till the time of his death and then bring back his subtle body to Fairy Land. At that time, he could be converted into a male Fairy and then could marry according to the Fairies' rules and live happily in Fairy Land.

All were satisfied with this verdict. Raslila went with Behari to his home and they lived happily till the time came for Behari to leave his body.

Raslila, with the *genie's* help, took Behari's subtle body and they went back to the Fairy Land. The king gave Behari nectar to drink which transformed him into a most handsome male Fairy. Then, according to the rules and traditions of the Fairies, once again Behari and Raslila got married.

He set free the *genie*. The *genie* was overjoyed and returned to his own genie land.

Behari and Raslila lived happily ever after in Fairy Land.

THE MONKEYS AND THE SPACE CRAFT

In the jungle near Ooty, there lived two monkeys. Their names were Mickey and Jackey. They were very close friends.

One night, after their dinner of a few bananas, they were both dozing on a branch of a tree when they saw a light emanating through the trees in a northerly direction. It was accompanied by a whirring sound.

Mickey and Jackey looked at each other in surprise, since all monkeys were curious, they decided to investigate.

They followed the sound and the direction of the light till they came to a small clearing in the jungle. What they saw amazed them. Hidden within the leaves of the tree, they looked on.

A round metallic object with small windows going round it had just made a landing from the skies. The whirring sound was coming from its engines and the light was shinning from both its headlamps.

The engines were shut off. The sound stopped. The lights were switched off. Now, only the lights inside remained.

Mickey and Jackey got down from the trees with great agility and ran across the clearing to where the spacecraft landed. They peered in through the windows with their mouths kept open in surprise. They saw something new. These were miniature human beings, not more than a foot off the ground. They were beautifully proportioned and their faces were angelic. They wore peculiar head gear with two antenae sticking out of it over their heads.

These little men and women were busy working on various machines. One of them, who appeared to be their leader was giving directions. A light was suddenly beamed onto Mickey and Jackey. They were lifted off their feet and when they opened their eyes again, they found themselves in a chamber inside the spacecraft. The leader was facing them.

Mickey and Jackey were paralysed with fear. It showed in their eyes. Then they heard a voice, "Don't be scared - we will not harm you." They looked around, the leader was addressing them. "you are surprised that I can speak to you in your language," he said. "we have the ability to understand and converse with any creature of the universe. This science has been developed on our planet."

Mickey and Jackey gathered their wits and asked,"where do you come from?" He answered,"we come from a planet called Zora millions of light years away. The last time we visited the Earth was long ago in Earth years. Are you earthlings?"

Mickey,"No, we are monkeys, a species of animals that lives in the jungle. Human beings live in cities and villages outside the jungles and they come and kill us and catch other animals."

The leader said,"I see. That means that the earthlings have destroyed their civilisation and have become primitive again. The last time we came, our records show that the earth had a very advanced society."

Jackey asked, "How could that be possible?"

The leader, "On the earth human beings are engaged in wars. When the civilisation advances, the weapons of mass destruction also become very sophisticated. In such a war the earthlings must have destroyed everything. Now, a new cycle of advancement has begun."

Mickey said,"Don't you have wars on your planet?"

The leader,"No, we have no wars. With the advancement of science, we developed our spiritual natures also. This understanding of God and His creation stops is from destruction."

Then the leader addressed his men and women. He instructed them to get ready for the journey back to their own planet.

The leader to Mickey and Jackey, "Don't mention our adventure to the human beings. We have learnt whatever we wanted to and now we are going back. This planet is too primitive to be of any use to us."

Mickey explained, "We can't tell the human beings because they will not understand us."

The leader said, "So they have lost the capacity to understand the other creatures on their own planet. Well, I suppose till the earthlings learn to develop their spiritual natures simultaneously with the scientific advancement, this is going to be their fate. Goodbye. Back to your jungle and live in peace."

The next instant Mickey and Jackey found themselves outside on the clearing next to the spacecraft. Then the engines and lights were switched on. The round object lifted above the ground and the next minute it was touching the sky. Then it disappeared from their sight.

Mickey and Jackey rubbed their eyes and wondered whether they had dreamt all of it?

COWARD

Every person has something to confess, something buried deep within the consciousness, something which one would rather forget but this does not happen. It keeps bubbling to the surface as a cork rises in water and floats to the top.

One such instance keeps surfacing. It batters at me and leaves me mentally and physically drained. Being constantly reminded of it proves that I have not been able to forget the events which have set this chain of consequences into motion.

How old was I then? Twenty-five. Another twenty-five years have gone by. The passage of time, they say, makes one forget. The reverse has happened. As the years go by, the intensity of remorse and guilt has heightened. I am unable to shake off this mantle of cowardice which has been bestowed upon me by my conscience. "Coward," says a voice from within. I surround myself with people. I try to lose myself. It is of no avail. The inner voice mocks.

Where should I go? What should I do? I have taken to social service, to helping needy women and children. I have given donations. I have actively participated in the construction of institutions for the destitute. I throw myself into these social activities hoping that my conscience will relent and say that you have made up for your lapse. It does not happen. I go to temples, churches, mosques. I beg for forgiveness. I beg for respite from this self-torture. I try to rationalise. I argue but nothing helps. What atonement is required of me, I ask? I will do anything, I say. Release me from this Hell, I pray. There is silence.

It happened so many years ago and yet it is so finely etched in my consciousness. It was a lovely day in December. There was a cold crispness in the air which bit through the woollens and made one aware that it was mid-winter. My office was situated in the middle of the city. I remember glancing at the wall clock more than once, impatiently willing it to strike the five O'clock dong. I had an appointment with a dear friend of mine, a school friend. I was to spend the night with her in the old rambling country house. The impatience was further emphasised due to the fact that I had to board the 5.30 bus which take me twenty kilometres away to my destination.

The bus ride was relaxing. Looking out through the bus window, I remember the red glow of the setting sun. The countryside was bathed in an iridescent hue. The wind ruffled my hair. The old man seated beside me requested that the window shutter be pulled down.

The bus came to a halt. I got out. The house was a few hundred yards away. I remember pulling my coat around me for additional warmth as I started walking towards the house.

The house was a huge old-time mansion which had been constructed during the British reign and, as such, had overtones of British architecture. The fifty-foot drive was lined on either side by tall and graceful Ashoka trees. The place had a rustic majesty about it. The whole area was covered with a mantle of silence. This was the only house within a mile.

As I walked forward, I was becoming aware of music penetrating the silence. I knew Sheila was behind this. She had always been a music addict. It was light jazz.

I walked onto the porch, up the steps and pulled at the brass knocker. After a duration of may be thirty seconds, the door was flung open. Sheila stood before me dressed in casual denims and a chunky light blue sweater. We embraced. We had met after an interval of three years. She drew me into the warmth of the lounge and then into the drawing room where the music played.

I remembered the homely warmth of the room. The comfortable softness of the huge sofa as I sank into its vastness. This is when it struck me that I was chilled to the bone.

Sheila prepared some hot steaming coffee. It was very welcome. Cupping it in both hands, I sipped from the mug.

Sheila had put on some weight but it suited her. I remarked on it and her pleased laugh rippled through the room. We started chatting, trying to fill in all the gaps.

Sheila had always been very vivacious talker and, as usual, she had me totally engrossed in her narrative about her adventures in Rome, Paris and various other famous cities of Europe. I recall the twinge of envy which I experienced. My existence was so mundane compared to hers.

She talked, I listened. Suddenly she jumped up, ran to the sideboard, picked up a packet and dropped it into my lap saying that it was for me.

A most exquisitely carved silver bracelet lay against the velvet of the case. I still have it with me. I had put it in my coat pocket after thanking her. I have not worn it because I cannot bear to look at it, but neither could I throw it away. It remains with me, a symbol of my guilt.

At 9.30 pm we had our dinner. The silverware glinted in the candle light. The beautifully arranged flowers added beauty and colour to the dining table. Sheila had always been fond of the good things of life. She had done everything herself. The servants had been sent away earlier. We were the only two inmates of this huge mansion.

After dinner she showed me to my room. In the middle of it stood a four-poster bed. I sank into its softness and drew the quilt over me. Her room was at the other end of the corridor, two rooms away from me.

The softness and the warmth were instrumental in making me fall asleep instantly. I remember I woke up with a jolt. My heart was thumping and my hands were cold. There was silence but I was sure that I had heard something. I recall lying in bed speculating on whether to investigate or not. I was afraid.

After a moment or so, I slipped out of bed, put on some clothes and ventured into the corridor. The light in Sheila's room was on. I do not know what stopped me from calling her.

I was in front of her door, which was slightly open. Voices drifted towards me. I peeped in. The scene which unfolded in front of my eyes puzzled me. Sheila was being confronted by two men. She obviously knew them. She was also very scared. I did not know whether to enter or remain where I was. I chose the latter. I could not hear the conversations but the men were annoyed and Sheila was desperately pleading. She motioned them to leave. Her back was towards them as she came forward to open the door. One of the men hit her on the head with his fist. She crumpled to the floor. The other drew a nylon cord from his pocket, wrapped it around her neck and gave it a jerk. I heard a distinct snap. Sheila was dead. My mind registered that, even as I was trembling partly from the cold and partly from the fear which engulfed me.

I ran down the corridor to my room and hid in the closet. I was terrified that they would discover my presence. I remained there, crouched in an uncomfortable position for what seemed an eternity. The room turned grey and I realised that dawn was extending its fingers.

I remember putting on my coat and running out of the house through the kitchen door. I was still gripped with fear. The only coherent thought my brain could formulate was to get away from the house, away to safety.

The first bus arrived; I climbed abroad and paid for my ticket. I was in a trance. The fear was like a knot at the base of my throat. My stop came. The conductor patted my shoulder. I jumped up, suppressing a hysterical scream from crossing my lips.

I got out and walked to my flat which was two streets away. I let myself in.

Everything was as I left it. The door closed behind me with a click. This is when the enormity of what had happened penetrated my fear-laden mind. I shook with grief. My sobs were checked when I heard a voice say "Coward". That was the beginning.

I had run away. I had not lifted a finger to help my friend. I knew that if I had showed myself to those men, they would have killed me. I knew that I would have been helpless against them. But I had run away, I had not even had the courage to inform the police. I had run away and my conscience had labelled me a coward. There was no escape.

My mind rationalised. My conscience rebuked. My mind said anybody would have behaved the same way. It was the only sensible thing to do. The self-torture had begun.

The evening newspapers carried the news. I read the newspaper avidly and remember with shame the relief I felt when none of them mentioned my visit. I was scared that the police might hold me responsible. Nothing happened. The culprits were not caught.

Days turned into months and months into years. I did everything to redeem my one moment of fear, but it was useless. I could not shake the self-application of "COWARD". I was branded for life. I know now that I will carry this shame to my grave and maybe beyond. I carry the self-inflicted tag rest of my life on my shoulders like a burden. I must live with this shame which burns within me and eats away at my insides like a canker. My only prayer is for deliverance from this guilt. My only hope is that my maker is more forgiving than I.

MEMORIES

Memories flit across the mind's eye. I sit before the bay window in my favourite rocking chair. The gentle breeze ruffles my peppered hair. The chirping of the birds awaking to the rising morning sun sounds pleasant to the ears. I sip my tea and allow the past to unfold.

I like being alone. I am a loner, people call me eccentric. I gave up worrying about social opinions and taboos a long, long while back. My life is settled. I am at peace.

What a price one has to pay for a word that sounds as simple as "peace". Being a woman in India is not an easy thing. She has innumerable handicaps to fight against. I have always enjoyed being a woman in spite of the hardships encountered. If God ever gave me a chance to decide, I would opt over and over again for a woman's role. It is so much more colourful, dramatic and full of ups and downs which a man does not experience. To understand the sensitive nuances and the finer points of a woman's existence are simply beyond the scope of his comprehension. Life, after all, is a stage, as Shakespeare so aptly put it. We are the players. Why not choose a role which requires more expertise?

The marriage ceremony unfolds like a disjointed video film - I hear the Sanskrit *mantras* being recited in a low monotonous drone. I did not know what they meant. The Pandit reciting them was equally ignorant of their meaning. This is where our love for baseless tradition has brought us. We know nothing but we like to talk a great deal on matters we have no knowledge about. The significance of the Hindu marriage is, I am sure, unknown to the majority.

The stranger sitting beside me was pronounced my husband. I wondered, why him? And why not anybody else? Personally, it made no difference. I did not even know him.

He made a very bad husband. He was uncaring. He was excessively possessive and unreasonably suspicious. Besides all these wonderful qualities, he was a very cruel and selfish man.

I wanted to leave him. The arguments expounded against such a heinous step were many: he is good looking; he comes from a good family background; he is financially well-settled—what more can a woman possibly want? (Love and consideration, I thought). Men are like this. A woman must put up with her Lord and Master's whims and fancies uncomplainingly. After all, he feeds and clothes her.

I left him despite all the very good reasons given for not doing so. The storm did not abate. It worsened.

The men, upon hearing that I was a divorcee, presumed that I was easily available. The majority of the men I encountered were very closely related to Ravan and seemed to share his mentality. The ordinary housewives were suspicious that I may have designs on their husbands. There were a number of unpleasant experiences.

The one thing which kept me going was my firm belief that there was good in life. There were good people around and life was worth living and fighting for. During my childhood, I remember my parents telling me that God takes care of us—if we pray to Him, help comes.

I prayed with an intensity which people termed as crazy. Help came. I got the strength from within to accept my circumstances bravely and honestly. Then came peace and the realisation that one must have the courage of one's own convictions in life. One must learn to be true to one's own ideal, whatever that may be.

I wanted to work and I did. I enjoyed travelling and did so whenever I could afford it. I wanted to become a member of a club in my right, so I did. I did whatever I wanted to, but holding on the feet of the Almighty for support and sustenance. My only prayer being, "Give me the enough courage to endure my circumstances calmly and cheerfully without straying from the right path."

The years rolled on. Relatives clamoured, "Get married again. Settle down. A woman cannot manage alone."

I was open to marriage. I wanted a man to care for me. I accepted that. The one thing which was also very clear in my mind was that I should want to marry him. He should want me also as his wife and partner in life. We should want to share our lives. I was not going to settle for less.

I did not compromise. Many men wanted me because I was a good looking woman. I did not want them. No man did I come across for who it seemed worth the trouble of giving up my independence. They also did not try to make me change my mind. I did not change it.

The sunset of my years is ahead of me. I am at peace within, for not having compromised. People call me an idealist and a fool. May be I was, may be I am. A fool at peace is a far more desirable state than a fool in agony.

The second cup of tea comes to an end. I shake my head, the memories disappear. The thought which surfaced was — "I wish our Indian men would be more realistic about what they want in a wife. She is a human being. She cannot be perfect. This wanting of a *Devi* in the guise of a woman is the effect of centuries of religious conditioning. It has seeped into the innermost core of our being."

More and more marriages are breaking-up in our times. Women have changed through education and exposure and an evolving environment. It is a world phenomenon. Unfortunately, our men have not changed. They still remain the way their forefathers were, steeped in mythological lore and superstitious rubbish about their superiority and wanting women to pay homage to them. If the men do not become more sensitive to the sufferings of women, they will suffer. It is all inter-linked after all. Men want their wives to be Sitas and Savitris, but how many of them even think in terms of being husbands like Rama and Satyavan?

I have my breakfast to make and my dog, my constant loving companion, to feed. Let the younger generation take up the fight and the analysis. I have other things to attend to.

BLACK MAGIC OF BENGAL

The 'black magic' of Bengal was supposed to be very potent, and as the belief went, was practiced by a set of *Tantrics*. *Tantrics,* according to popular belief, are worshippers of *shakti* and this particular form of worship was kept very secret.

Now, in the deep recesses of a remote village in Medieval Bengal there lived a *Tantric* who had perfected in the art of 'black magic' and he practiced it.

It was believed that he could, by the power of his *mantras*, turn human beings into any form of an animal. He chanted potent *mantras* and then drove a nail into the person's head. People were terrified of him. He had turned a number of unfortunate humans into animals and kept them confined.

Then one day, a very beautiful woman lost her way and came to his cottage. The *Tantric* saw her and at once had evil designs and wanted her as his wife. He asked her but the woman was already married and wanted to return to her husband. The evil man would not permit her to do that and by the power of his magic, drove a nail into her head and changed her into a beautiful bird. He kept her confined in a golden cage.

Now, her husband who loved her very much set out to search for her. The only information he could gather was that she was last seen in the vicinity of the *Tantric*. People warned him and told him that she was also probably being held by this evil magician.

Her husband was a brave man and was determined to find his wife and release her from the hold of this evil man if she was with him. He decided to approach the *Tantric* and ask for employment. He got the job of a domestic help because the *Tantric* was confident that nobody could harm him.

A very long time went by and Rajat, which was the name, the magician had given him, could find no clue of his wife. Then one day he happened to open a door which was always locked. There he saw this bird in the golden cage. He went up to the cage and was certain that he had to find out the secrecy about the bird. By now Rajat had gained the confidence of the *Tantric* due to his honest services and obedient ways.

That night, Rajat gave the magician a little more to drink than normal. When the evil man was in a vulnerable mood and wanted to boast of his exploits, Rajat questioned him. The *Tantric* told him how he could convert humans into animals and how they could be released from this spell. He also told Rajat about this woman whom he wanted to marry, but she did not agree, so he had confined her in a cage in the form of a bird. In his drunken stupor, the magician sought Rajat's help to marry her.

Rajat at once ran to the room where his wife was confined, and started chanting the *mantras,* disclosed to him and took out the nail buried in the bird's head. Lo and behold, the form of the bird disappeared and his wife was before him. They both did not waste any time and ran out of the house. But then his wife told Rajat that the magician had to be destroyed and the only way to do this was to burn him.

They both set fire to his cottage. The magician perished in the fire and when he died, the effect of his magic died with him. All the other humans whom he had converted into animals regained their normal form and thanked Rajat and his wife profusely. That is how the menace of this *Tantric* magician practicing 'black magic' was removed. It was all because of Rajat's bravery.

Presence of mind in the face of adversity, tenacity of purpose and love for his wife was what made this impossible possible.